Rupture and Repair

A Therapeutic Process with EMDR Therapy

Esly Regina Carvalho, Ph.D.

TraumaClinic Edições

TraumaClinic Edições

2018

Rupture and Repair

A Therapeutic Process with EMDR Therapy

Esly Regina Carvalho, Ph.D.

TraumaClinic Edições

2018

Rupture and Repair: A Therapeutic Process with EMDR Therapy

Series: Clinical Strategies in Psychotherapy, Volume 4

Originally published in Portuguese, 2017

ISBN-13: 978-1-941727-65-2
ISBN-10: 1-941727-65-4

Cover Art: Claudio Ferreira da Silva e Ederson Oliveira

TraumaClinic Edições

SEPS 705/905 Ed. Santa Cruz, sala 441
70.390-055 Brasília, DF, Brasil

www.plazacounselingservices.com
www.traumaclinicedicoes.com.br
vendas@traumaclinicedicoes.com.br
+55 61 3443 8447

Special thanks to "Armando" for letting us tell his story.

Dedicated to...

Vô Jerônymo, my Portuguese grandfather, who was born in 1892. When I was fifteen years old, he taught me to touch-type: typing without looking at the keys. As a result, I have precise patient notes…and wonderful memories of him coming home with his pockets full of *bonbons*.

Table of Contents

Presentation

Many people are curious about the psychotherapy process and how it works. Some are mental health professionals who are directly or indirectly involved with a population who find them for treatment of specific issues such as anxiety, depression, phobias, fears, or traumas. Even though many professionals have gleaned important information during their university studies, and have completed further education courses, it is not always possible to learn the daily process of psychotherapy without actually doing it. This book offers an inside view of how psychotherapy can be done with EMDR.

Those without professional training will also benefit from this book. Some people are just plain curious. Others may consider the possibility of going to therapy, but are reluctant to submit to an unknown experience.

This book will take the reader from the beginning to the end of a psychotherapeutic process with EMDR therapy. We will attain a clinical history and accompany the client, step-by-step and session-by-session, all the way to the end of treatment. Our client, Armando (not his real name), has authorized us to publish his story for the benefit of others. We will highlight the different moments of the six "Rs" of the therapeutic process: *Revision, Rupture, Reprocessing, Repair, Reconciliation, and Resolution.*

EMDR therapy is known not only for its scientific and measurable results, but also for its focus on clear and specific targets. As my friend, Santiago Jácome from Ecuador says, *"We don't do psychotherapy like in the olden days."* With this therapeutic revolution comes a real paradigm shift, for it is now possible to focus on specific issues that afflict the patient. By applying the eight phases of EMDR therapy, we can see, little by little, how difficult memories that had people stuck can be resolved at an accelerated pace.

An interesting aspect of EMDR therapy is that it does not require that patients speak extensively about their traumatic experiences. This can be an enormous relief for those who are ashamed—or terrified—about sharing the details of what happened to them. In this sense, EMDR therapy preserves a patient's privacy.

Another interesting change in my clinical practice has been the fact that more and more men have explored this kind of therapy. It is more logical, linear, and does not require them to necessarily share their feelings. Many men feel more comfortable going into a therapeutic process that has a clear beginning, middle, and end. I have a male friend who says, *"I don't believe in psychologists, but I send people to your clinic because I see that the therapy you do has an ending, and it ends well."*

So, we decided to share this process with our readers. We are grateful to Armando, who has allowed us to tell his story with the hope that it will take others from rupture to repair.

What is EMDR Therapy?[1]

EMDR – Eye Movement Desensitization and Reprocessing

Tamara got up from the table, took a deep breath, and went up the escalator for the first time in her life. Helen arrived at the office and discussed how she had been able to undergo an MRI without any anxiety or medication. Rodrigo returned to driving for the first time since the car accident that took his friend's life. Patricia was finally able to have blood exams after losing her fear of needles. John's comment about having his house burglarized and six members of his family held at gunpoint for four hours—an experience that had him so incapacitated he hadn't been able to work for a year—was simply, *"Oh, that's just a story to tell at happy hour."*

EMDR

What do all these people have in common? They have submitted themselves to a new and revolutionary approach called EMDR—Eye Movement Desensitization and Reprocessing—which was discovered in 1987 in the United States by Dr. Francine Shapiro. Since then, more than 100,000 therapists have been trained worldwide in EMDR, representing a paradigm shift in psychotherapy.

---

[1] This chapter is taken from another book by this author, *Healing the Folks Who Live Inside.*

If we understand that traumas, nightmares, and bad memories of adverse situations are stored in a maladaptive form in the brain, then we can begin to understand how EMDR can reprocess these fears, phobias, terrors, and anxieties connected to painful memories that keep victims trapped by the ghosts of their past. This is accomplished by the integration of reprocessed information that was once in separate parts of the brain. In an accelerated and adaptive manner, EMDR seems to "imitate" what happens to people as they go through the REM (Rapid Eye Movement) phases of the sleep cycle. This is the phase when the brain processes daily life and stores it in an adaptive form, then transforms it into past memory. For reasons that are not totally understood, in some situations people are not able to process this information in a normal and healthy manner. Perhaps this is the origin of nightmares, startle responses, intrusive and obsessive thoughts, or post-traumatic stress disorder (PTSD) and its consequences. In some cases, people can develop Dissociative Identity Disorder (DID) as a result of chronic, repetitive, and constant traumas (such as incest) that occur during childhood.

To apply EMDR, the psychotherapist needs to be duly trained in accredited courses where EMDR theory (as well as the practice of the eight phases of EMDR therapy) is taught along with three-pronged (past, present, and future) protocol. Trained therapists learn how to evaluate the indication (or lack thereof) for EMDR therapy, how to develop a treatment plan, and how to conceptualize the diagnosis and treatment according to Adaptive Information Processing, which is the theoretical basis for EMDR.

Beginning with the first phase, the patient shares his or her history, and the therapist then identifies the adverse situations, traumas, and painful memories that may become targets for future reprocessing. In the second phase, the therapist will help the patient install positive resources that will enable the patient to face difficult moments within or outside the sessions. Different kinds of bilateral stimulation (visual, auditory, and tactile) are offered to the patient so that he or she can become familiar with them. In addition, the EMDR approach is explained to the client to obtain informed consent. In the third phase, we "open" the brain file that contains the difficult memory by asking for the image, beliefs, emotions, and sensations that are tied to it.

EMDR therapists use two measurements scales. The first is the SUDS (Subjective Units of Disturbance Scale), which measures disturbance. Therapists will often ask the patient, "On a scale of one to ten, where ten is the greatest disturbance that you can imagine and zero is no disturbance at all, how much disturbance do you feel when you think about that experience right now?" This allows the therapist to accompany the level of resolution of the experience while the bilateral stimulation is being applied. This scale was originally developed by Joseph Wolpe, who worked with desensitization, and developed the means to statistically evaluate subjective experiences.

The therapist also uses a second type of measurement when asking the client to think of an ideal situation in which the present experience has been totally resolved. The therapist asks, "On a scale of one to seven, where seven is completely true and one is completely false, how true do you feel the positive belief about this experience is to you when you think about it?" Francine Shapiro developed this second scale. It made it possible to accompany the resolution of the traumatic experience as it is processed and becomes more and more adaptive in nature.

Because of these measurements, it is possible to develop statistical designs for empirical research. Perhaps one of Dr. Shapiro's greatest contributions has been her insistence on research—which has led to the publication of over 200 scientific studies in peer-reviewed journals, and to a journal dedicated specifically to EMDR Research and Practice.[2] In 2010, EMDR was recognized and acknowledged as an evidence-based psychotherapeutic approach by the National Registry of Evidence-Based Programs and Practices (NREPP).[3] Today, EMDR efficacy is undeniable.

In the fourth phase, the therapist applies the bilateral stimulation that helps the brain reprocess the painful and/or traumatic memories. The bilateral stimulation reactivates the Adaptive Information Processing system, which was previously unable to fully process the experience, and therefore maladaptively stored the information. EMDR gives the brain a second chance to reprocess the traumatic memory, thus transforming it into an adaptive resolution.

Often, people will have intense emotional reactions while reprocessing. This should not surprise us, since past experiences come up in much the same way that they were stored. This does not mean that the person is being re-traumatized. It simply means that the negative content is being discharged.

---

[2] http://www.springerpub.com/product/19333196 retrieved March 16, 2013

[3] http://nrepp.samhsa.gov/ViewIntervention.aspx?id=199 retrieved March 16, 2013

On the other hand, intense abreactions can reach a tipping point since it is no longer an issue of reprocessing because the client may dissociate and the processing stops. The person's brain becomes unable to make the adaptive connections necessary to take the experience to an adequate resolution. We can say that with over-the-top emotions, some of the Inner Roles get scared and "flee" (dissociate again) to their frozen places to protect themselves. Through dissociation, they go to the place where they have the illusion of being protected (and pay a high price for this). But the survival strategy once again converts the situation into an ice cage.

Each traumatized role has aspects that are frozen and dissociated. When the client connects to this role, it triggers anything that was dysfunctionally stored. Often, these roles were frozen in childhood, a time when the person had fewer resources, options, or choices about how to deal with what was happening to her. Her "emotional circuits" got overloaded and dissociation was how she survived.

The fifth phase begins when the negative and painful memories have been reprocessed, because positive beliefs can be linked to the target memory the client is working on. It is as if the patient, having emptied out a glass of dirty water, can now fill that glass with clean water.

In the sixth phase, the client does a mental scan of his or her body to determine if there is any physical disturbance left, which is also processed with bilateral stimulation.

The session ends with the seventh phase, in which the client is given specific instructions about what to expect between sessions, how to contact the therapist if necessary, and how to take note of what happens to him during the coming week.

Finally, the eighth phase occurs when the client returns for the next session, and the therapist receives his or her feedback and evaluates the results from the previous session. This information will help the therapist build an ideal treatment plan.

As always, appropriate history-taking is essential to evaluate whether the client has an indication for this kind of psychotherapy, since there can be contraindications. Although the results can sometimes be amazing, these are not "miracle cures."

To process effectively, it is necessary for the patient to feel safe and secure. An important part of this security comes from the therapeutic relationship. If it is not possible to trust the person who will accompany us on our healing pilgrimage—and there may be terrifying parts along the road—then the patient will not surrender to the healing process. After all, there is a whole gallery of roles for which the Adult feels responsible—roles that need protection. If any of the inner roles don't feel safe and protected, or if they get scared, the process will not move forward.

This is one of the reasons we emphasize that love is what heals. Perhaps it sounds strange to talk about love in a psychotherapeutic context, but it is love and positive emotions that will give clients enough security and a sense of safety to board the ship of hope. It is the security of unconditional acceptance on the part of the therapist that will encourage the patients to take this trip inside of themselves to visit the wounded members of their Inner Gallery. This will allow them to be healed with these new psychotherapeutic tools; but without love, no one has the courage for the trip.

What is it about EMDR that makes it seem like a paradigm shift in psychotherapy? First of all, it is an approach that produces changes in the brain. Modern brain scans demonstrate the physical alterations that result from the application of EMDR.[4] The resolution of the painful experience is the result of the integration of neuronal information that is often dissociated in the brain networks where the traumatic information and the resources for healing are stored in separate hemispheres. Sometimes clients say that they "don't have words to explain what happened," and this is literally true because the unprocessed memory is dissociated from the part of the brain that can attribute words and meaning to what they have experienced. Only after it is reprocessed can the client report an integrated explanation to his or her experience.

Secondly, talking about their negative experiences is not necessary for clients to heal. For 120 years, psychotherapists have been taught that patients must talk about their painful experiences to change (beginning with Breuer's revolutionary "talking cure"). However, with EMDR, talking can be kept to a minimum, since reprocessing the memory in the brain is what will heal the patient. For some clients who are shy, too embarrassed, or too ashamed to talk about some of their experiences—such as sexual abuse or rape—this aspect of EMDR is a godsend. It allows clients the opportunity to privately reprocess their memories.

---

[4] Lansing, K., Amen, D., Hanks, C., Rudy, L. (2005) High Resolution Brain SPECT Imaging and EMDR in Police Officers With PTSD. *The Journal of Neuropsychiatry and Clinical Neurosciences* (17)

Perhaps the greatest joy we have as EMDR therapists is hearing our patients tell us things like this when they have finished reprocessing their memories:

"It's over. Now it's distant. It's in the past."

When they return in the following sessions, they say:

"I remember, but it doesn't bother me anymore."

"I can't remember it like I did before."

"It's not clear and crisp anymore. The picture is cloudy."

"Is it normal to have so much relief in such a short amount of time?"

"People say and do those things that bothered me so much before, and now it doesn't matter anymore."

"I'm sleeping well for the first time in years!"

"Hmm. How strange. I haven't thought about that at all during the week."

"Funny, this EMDR stuff...it's as if it never happened to me. It's like EMDR put that experience in a place where it never happened. It's like I used to look at a room filled with old stuff and now it's all gone. Everything is organized and I can't even remember what it was like before!"

"This EMDR is magic!"

Revision

All psychotherapy begins with a good reason for seeking help. Usually, something happened that triggered the need for therapy. Most people don't go simply because they have a deep longing to do so; they often choose treatment because they believe that not going could be worse.

We begin by taking Armando's clinical history, and the reasons that brought him to therapy. Armando will then tell us his story. It is important to take as complete a history as possible, and not just focus on the initial trigger that brings someone to therapy. This is where we begin to uncover the secrets of eventual therapeutic resolution.

Sometimes patients find it strange that I ask them about their childhood, family of origin, their difficulties, painful memories, accidents, illnesses, and surgeries, but it is from life's fractures that we find the secrets that lead us to healing. These distant memories that were not properly processed block present-day solutions in mysterious—or sometimes obvious—ways, once the connection can be made.

It is in the history-taking phase that we learn to hear the "ruptures" that will become the therapeutic goals. The first session is essential to put together a good treatment plan.

Perhaps this is the place to make the brutally honest observation that few of us health professionals in Brazil learn how to develop a treatment plan. Unfortunately, this is not logically taught in our universities. I remember, with a certain terror, when patients would ask me, *"So, how long do you think this will take?"* I didn't have an answer. I didn't have any idea what kind of a reply to give them. The standard response back then was to say that it had taken a long time to get the way they were, so it would also take a long time to undo the damage.

Treatment plan? Psychotherapists were known for working with their "intuition." In spite of the fact that I still have a profound trust in my intuition, it does not put together a treatment plan, nor does it justify the ongoing continuation of a therapeutic process without concrete results.

Today, I work in a very different way. There are treatment plans. There are clear therapeutic goals. There are measurements that help us decide when therapy is done. The turnover rate is now much higher because patients get well more quickly and then leave. (That's a great problem!) When I first began working with EMDR therapy I had concerns about the number of clients that began to leave. But it didn't take long for a waiting list to develop because these former clients would tell their friends and relatives about a therapy that "really works."

Another interesting element is that the profile of our clients changed. About 90% of our patient-load was female, but now it is closer to 50%, a number that better reflects our population. I'm not sure how to explain it, but I believe the fact that men don't have to share intimate details, talk a lot, or discuss their feelings is part of it. Perhaps it is because EMDR therapy is a logical therapy with clear goals and concrete results, and that attracts men.

In *Revision,* you will meet our patient, Armando, to whom we will dedicate the rest of our book. We will hike together through his therapeutic path. Once in a while, I will interrupt to make a comment or observation about something that is happening or discuss the process. But most of the time, I'll let him tell his own story.

First Session: Armando's Story

I have always been shy and I've had to learn to overcome it. I hold an executive position in a public organization where I often have to speak in public. It is really hard to speak to a roomful of strangers. It comes from the need I have to say the right thing, and use the most intelligent words. Maybe it comes from something in my past, where I had a phobia about speaking. I always felt I had to say the perfect thing.

Yesterday, I was at a forum, with some judges and lawyers. I do all right with a small group, but if it starts to get a little bigger…I get scared that the sound of my voice won't come out. There's a ball in my throat and I'm afraid my speech will get stuck. I get nervous thinking that it could happen in a group like that, so I wind up not saying anything, even though I know the subject matter well. I want to speak up and I'm not able. Yesterday I didn't say a thing.

Therapist: Do you remember when all of this began?

I remember scenes in kindergarten, sitting with the kids at recess. I don't remember the exact moment it began. Shyness has always been a part of my personality. I have a history of exacerbated anxiety. My father committed suicide when I was an adolescent. He was a real hero-father, but he was also an alcoholic. I often had to carry my dad to bed at night because I was the oldest son. He was violent with my mom. He had some psychiatric problems. One day he put a bullet through his head. I didn't see it, but it happened close to my house, at a park. People I didn't know found him. The maid who had worked with us for many years was the first to learn the news. When he left home, I was the last person with whom he spoke. He had a bag. He was on leave from work, which is why he was at home. He just said, *"I'm going for a walk in the park."*

On Sundays, he wouldn't drink because he had to go back to work on Monday. He would only drink on weekends. I looked in a desk, and found his note. *"Take good care of the children."* I thought he had just left home.

I was getting ready to go to a military school. I studied at a boarding school for three years. It was far away from home and it was hard to be away at that time. My dad, drunk on weekends, would say that if something happened to him, I was to take care of the family. I was determined to do things right, so it was really hard, but I stayed away from home [after my dad's death].

What made things easier was the fact that I did really well at school. I was a good student and did well in sports, too. I had exceptional grades. My dad had gone to a naval academy, and he influenced me to go to military school. I had already made that decision before he died. I was able to pass the entrance exams and left to study in a distant city. I thought I was wasting my youth inside that school. It would take seven years to become a military officer. So, I gave it up. I went back and did college instead. In a nearby city, I met the woman who would eventually become my wife. We later transferred to this same city, where we live now, when I still worked for a private company. I wound passed the exams to become a civil servant.

I thought about going back to school, but I wound up going into the political arena. I like the world of politics.

T: Tell us a little bit about your family of origin.

I am the oldest of five siblings. Another little tragedy…some years ago one of my sisters died of cancer. I became a donor in an attempt to save her life. Two years after the transplant, she passed away. She was 35 and left behind three little kids. The loss of my sister was very painful.

My mother is a true warrior, an overcomer. I call her on Father's Day. She never paid a bill her whole life [before my father's death]. She was a teacher and my dad took care of everything. She really struggled after he died. Two years after he passed away, she found another person and spent twenty years with him, until he died. He was very respectful. I was kind of jealous about it for a while, but when I think back, he was really an exceptional guy. He was very good to my mother.

I've been away from home a long time now. I met a lady who became my wife when I was very young. Years later, we met again. We don't have children yet, but we hope to have a half-dozen! I know it's a lot of responsibility.

My mother and my brother-in-law (who was married to the sister who passed away) always had their ups and downs. A few years before my sister died, they went to live with my mom because they needed a larger support system. He has family in another state, and they offered him the chance to change jobs. A year after my sister passed away, he went there to work. That was really hard for my mom, and for all of us. The children were small. Today, they still spend vacations with their grandmother.

T: What would you like to accomplish in therapy? What are some of the things you would like to resolve?

I would like to feel more at ease with myself; not as worried about dealing with unknown groups of people. I would also like to get rid of this phobia. But I haven't had a panic attack in a long time because the medication controls it really well.

My dad used to hit my mom when he drank. He would turn into a different person. I would restrain him. Once I came home really late. I was a high-performance athlete, and we got stuck in traffic on the way home from a game. He was waiting for us with a club in his hand, ready to beat my mother. He would slap her and stuff. These fights really bothered me a lot. Weekends were not good. It was a huge relief when he would sleep through Saturdays. There was a time when my mom said she was going to leave him, but I said I was going to stay with my dad. She wound up staying. I was about 10 or 11 at the time. We didn't have any financial difficulties because my dad was a civil servant. When he died, the apartment we lived in got paid off and my mom received a pension.

When I wanted to leave boarding school, after my father's death, my mom had to sign the authorization slip. She didn't let me leave, though. Looking back, I think it was a sensible decision on her part.

Later, I went off to college. I had a lot of panic attacks those first years. At the time, I didn't have a lot of information about this. I would be out somewhere, and all of a sudden, I just knew that I *had* to go home. For a while, this really put the brakes on my life. My mom was really worried about it. Psychotherapy didn't help me much. I did better with the medication, an antidepressant and an anxiolytic. That really saved me. I couldn't even leave the house or go on the road without the fear of having a panic attack. I couldn't catch a flight. Later, I was able to get off the meds. Now I can usually stay off of them for the most part, but in a pinch, I still take them. When I went to work in this new department, I was so anxious that I wound up taking the meds almost every day.

Like I said before, I was very shy at school, introspective. I had friends, a small group of them. I remember that they did a theater piece at school. I definitely don't have any acting chops! In the piece, the teacher made me one of the birds because I was the best student. But I did it without any problems. My difficulty was speaking in front of the class. At military school and at the end of high school, I wound up being a really popular guy.

Ten years ago, I became an evangelical Christian. My mother went the route of the charismatic Catholics.

I was really good at sports from a very young age. Perhaps that's why I had a kind of arrogance. Maybe it explains why I care so much about what people think of me. I feel like people are always evaluating me. It is important for me to feel this acceptance, where people say that I am the best. Intelligent. That causes some problems for me. My body feels it and my throat gets blocked. I'm afraid I won't have enough air and won't be able to finish speaking.

My father was always evaluating us. He was critical and rigid. My mother also had high expectations for us. Perhaps that's why I wasn't a troublesome child. My dad required good behavior from us. He was my reference regarding issues of integrity. On one hand, his death brought a certain relief, even though there was so much pain and fear. On the other hand, he left a gap in my life. For example, I didn't have anyone to teach me to drive.

But my wife and I have now been married for more than five years, and we live like lovebirds.

The therapist set up the initial treatment plan with the patient's input and the following therapy goals. As the therapist shared the plan, the patient made additional comments.

T: I think it would be important for us to work on the following issues, Armando.

1. People who are raised in an alcoholic home have to learn to deal with the lack of predictability regarding the state of the alcoholic person: whether they will come home drunk or sober, for example. So a child develops a special antenna for this. The tendency is to also maintain a certain level of heightened anxiety as a result of the fact that one never really knows what is going to happen.

This lack of predictability also keeps people from having a routine, something that is very important in the life of a child. Follow-through on clear expectations brings stability and security to one's life. This is usually lacking in a home where one of the parents is an alcoholic or has some other form of addiction.

2. Very few go through the experience of a family suicide without some residual consequences. This is an issue that deeply affects people. So we will certainly need to work on this, especially since you were the last person in your family to see your dad alive. You were the one who found the note as well.

3. Death leaves its mark. To lose a sister at such a young age is difficult, especially since you quite literally gave your blood (transplant) so she could live.

Armando: That's very true. I was the donor. When the cancer came back, the medulla didn't function anymore and she died. I was a brother who always kept picking on her. As we aged, we got to be good friends, so I feel like I missed out on that. I resent it, but I think I'm dealing well with it all.

T: Well, we can check on it during our process.

4. You also said that you often feel like you have to be perfect. This high level of expectation for yourself is not only problematic, but it also contributes to the anxiety attacks. People who feel like this won't allow themselves to make mistakes. This is probably part of the performance anxiety that brings you to therapy.

5. Of course, there is also the phobia, which is what pushed you to make this appointment.

Armando: Yes, this phobia… I remember when I was in the university… the panic. I went to a party with some friends one night and had to go back home. Situations like that would frequently happen to me. I would go out, but for some reason, I would have to leave and go home. On the way back, it would go away and I would be fine. I just had to get out of that situation

T: So, this is the treatment plan. If you would like to move forward with therapy, we can start next week.

A: Great.

Goals and the Treatment Plan

Comments:

Notice how it was possible to acquire a lot of information about Armando's life in the short space of an hour. The initial treatment plan or proposal—which may need adjustments and some fine-tuning—had five clear goals. If we were to offer a timeframe for treatment, I would say that we would need about 5-8 sessions for each goal, even though we might need fewer sessions for some (such as his sister's death). Other goals that were more complex (alcoholic home) might need additional sessions. Even though we suspected that his sister's death would probably rate high on the intensity scale, it did not bring with it the complexity that living in an alcoholic home does. The prognosis for the duration of therapy has more to do with the *complexity* of the issues involved than their *intensity*. Despite the fact that Armando mentioned that his sister's death had been resolved, it is always good to "check it out."

His father's suicide was a non-negotiable issue in terms of the treatment plan. We will see in the development of the therapy process how important it was to go back to this event that cut through his young life.

The trigger that brought Armando to therapy was his fear of public speaking, but knowing that this kind of anxiety attack usually has a foot in the past, it would be of paramount importance to work on the targets of his youth to remediate the present limitations that Armando presented. This would presumably also help develop better public performance as well. Anxiety can kill the prospect of a good performance. It is the feeling of being in danger, a knot in one's stomach, that sometimes shows up without any apparent explanation.

Armando would need to resolve that to perform better in public.

The Therapeutic Process

Most therapeutic processes have three moments: Diagnosis, Healing or Treatment, and Learning.

Diagnosis

I did my professional training in Brazil back when giving people a diagnosis had fallen out of style. We had learned that "labeling" a patient was unconscionable. This was in the time of Carl Rogers and humanism, B. F. Skinner and behaviorism, and psychoanalysis that infiltrated all forms of psychotherapy. The psychopathology we studied divided people into "normal," neurotic, or psychotic. The more common categories of mental illness focused on discerning whether the patient was a "hysteric" or phobic, or obsessive-compulsive, and so on—something that in practical terms turned out to be fairly useless. My impression at the time was that diagnostic categories didn't seem to be that important because we were never taught to really understand what had to happen for people to get well. I always considered this a great mystery, even taking into consideration that I was an exemplary student. I had passed very difficult university entrance exams that would have landed me in med school had I so desired. (However, I have only been able to deal with emotional blood. I still faint at the real thing!) I studied everything that was sent home and even sought out additional materials because I loved (and still love) my profession. But navigating psychotherapy and psychopathology was a challenge.

Perhaps one of the reasons that I was so attracted to Psychodrama—even before finishing my professional studies to become a psychologist in Brazil—was that it portrayed a very clear form of therapy with a beginning, middle, and end: the warm-up, the drama, and the sharing in each session. These were people's stories and I love stories! There was a crisis that had to be resolved in each session and a solution to be worked out. Every session was new and different. I specialized in Psychodrama and eventually became a trainer. But even so, the treatment plan and diagnosis eluded me.

In the years that I lived in the United States, I discovered a very different situation. It was important to give proper diagnoses where I worked, so we knew what kind of treatment to give the patients. I remember the expression, *"If you don't know where you are going, any road will take you there."*[5] I'd often felt that way as a student learning psychotherapy in Brazil. But in the US, things were very different. I remember the first time my clinical director asked me for my treatment plan. I froze. That was when the importance of getting all of this together really hit me.

Today, diagnostic manuals have solidified their importance, even in my own country. They help us evaluate patients in a more precise and functional manner. Psychotherapy has become more like medicine than philosophy. I still believe that we shouldn't "label" patients, but identifying what's wrong with a person helps guide us in their treatment plan. We need to have a working diagnosis, even if it is temporary or we have

---

[5] *If you don't know where you're going, any road will take you there.* Citation from Lewis Carroll in *Alice in Wonderland.*

to change or confirm it down the pike. As is often said, a well-defined problem is half-solved.

Healing or Treatment Phase

The second aspect of the psychotherapeutic process is the healing dimension. In a certain way, this begins even in the first session when we take the clinical history. A patient should feel safe with the way a therapist asks questions about his or her life, and how he or she proposes a treatment plan. This treatment phase is more than just making the patient feel better. We want to see realistic resolution regarding the difficulties that bring a client to therapy.

My friend and colleague, Ana Gomez, has the habit of explaining that clients usually come to therapy with one of three presenting requests. Some of them come to "fix things on the table." They usually have one very clear and well-defined issue that is bothering them; for example, they have a fear of flying. Perhaps they had a bad experience on a flight and from then on, they have been scared to fly. Sometimes these fears can keep people from doing things that are important to them. These patients usually have a clear memory about when the difficulty began. They just want to come in and solve the problem, At least that is their initial desire for therapy. (It does happen quite often that patients are amazed with the results of EMDR therapy and decide to continue therapy to resolve other issues, but initially they come in with one problem and want a fairly fast resolution.) Treating these folks with EMDR therapy will usually take five to eight sessions. Unless more complex issues arise, a specific phobia with a clear beginning point can usually be resolved in a short amount of time. Once the issue is resolved, the patient says goodbye and therapy is over. Sometimes he or she will come back with another specific difficulty, since there was such a positive result the first time around.

One of the interesting aspects of treating patients with EMDR therapy has been that there tends to be a higher turnover rate than with more traditional approaches. Since it is common for a patient to come in with a problem that they want resolved, and EMDR is pretty efficient in the resolution of clear-cut issues, patients leave therapy once this is settled. At the beginning of my practice with EMDR therapy, I would get a certain cold feeling in the pit of my stomach because patients left so quickly. But it wasn't long before I realized that even though these patients would leave in a shorter amount of time, they would talk with their friends and family about how this therapy really works. Soon there was a waiting list of clients. This became an interesting aspect of my clinical practice that continues to this day, and is now perceived as a sign of successful therapy.

Some people wonder if the issues theses clients face were actually resolved, since some of them will eventually come back to therapy. But even if the issue that brought them to therapy is settled, other things come up. Patients return because they know we already have their history, and they don't need to start all over with a new therapist. They understand how EMDR therapy works, and that it works for them. So they return with a new issue. Patients do come back, but rarely for the same reason that originally brought them to therapy. EMDR helps them get a definitive resolution if they are able to work through the whole network of triggers and memories that are involved. One of the scientific aspects of EMDR therapy is precisely the neurochemical transformation of difficult memories.

Ana Gomez says that other people come to therapy because they need to "fix a room." If we think of the personality as if it were a house, then some people come to fix a bigger issue than just a "table issue." It's not something quite so simple, like a fear of needles or a dog phobia. An aspect of the personality needs to be worked on.

For example, a young professional woman comes to therapy and explains that she has a very good job, her own home, a nice social life, and gets along fairly well with her family. However, she complains that she just can't choose good men to date. She would like to get into a stable relationship and get married. She will need to work on a whole aspect of her personality to understand and resolve her love life. We will need to learn what her relationship was like with her parents, especially her dad, her dating history and romantic relationships, what kind of complicated men she is unconsciously choosing to be with, and why she is in relationships that have no constructive future. This is what is meant by fixing up a room in the personality house, and it will usually take 6 to 12 months to understand it all, work on the memories that contribute to these unconscious choices, unlearn them, and develop a new ability to choose healthier relationships that have a chance at developing into marriage.

Ana also comments that there are also those who need to come in and "fix the whole house." These people's lives are pretty disorganized and dysfunctional. They need a kind of personality makeover. For these people, therapy could easily take one to two years, because it requires working on more complicated issues.

Finally, there are people with complex trauma and more serious diagnoses where therapy has to be done at a slower pace and with greater care. We know that the more difficult the diagnosis, the longer it will take to work on their issues in an orderly manner without destabilizing their life. There are also cases of serious dissociation and a loss of awareness during processing. Those clients need special care. Only EMDR therapists who are specialized in trauma and dissociation disorders tend to take on these clients because they may need to be in therapy even longer before beginning EMDR.

Learning Phase

As clients become better able to deal with their issues, they find a need to develop new responses and behaviors. At times, the simple resolution of the difficult memories that were holding people back is enough for appropriate and functional responses to spontaneously emerge. One of the interesting—and beautiful—aspects of EMDR therapy is how we often see patients tell us they are now able to do what was impossible for them a few weeks or months earlier. Even more surprising is when they didn't even realize it themselves. They only perceive the change when the therapist points it out to them. Trauma resolution often permits recovering that which is good. It is beautiful to see the person begin to live in a new dimension of functionality.

EMDR therapy isn't magic, and there may be a need to invest in learning new behaviors. Therapy may free people to lose their fear of math, but it won't teach them to do long division; it may heal them of their fear of public presentations but piano lessons and practice is still necessary for a lovely recital. Even social responses may need to be learned so that relationships can flow better. EMDR therapy may unblock certain difficulties, but the desired response still has to be learned.

Another interesting movement that tends to happen in the therapeutic process is the initial tendency and need to work on the old tapes: the memories and difficulties that are holding people back in their everyday lives. In the beginning, therapy is occupied with a lot of the childhood and adolescent experiences that left their mark on the adult. But as these issues are healed, the new direction is to work on what is presently happening, and their desires for the future. One of the signs that therapy is coming to an end is precisely the fact that the client is more involved in resolving—and learning—new responses, attitudes, and behaviors for their present-day lives.

The healing and learning phases tend to have an inverse relationship: there is not necessarily as much learning going on during the healing phase because the emphasis is on cleaning up the past. There isn't a lot of room yet for what's new. But as the past gets resolved, learning takes up more and more of the therapeutic process.

So, let's go back to Armando's story so we can see how this process plays out.

Rupture

Second session: one week later.

Armando arrived at the session and we exchanged the usual niceties. He had already received the general explanations about EMDR therapy in his initial interview.

In this session, we began to structure the first target to be treated with eye movements. (Note to EMDR therapists: I purposely delayed identifying the Positive Cognition several times until we got to Phase 5, after the Negative Cognition had been desensitized. Sometimes it was difficult to pick it up in the initial round of Phase 3.)

Therapist: I like to start the work of healing our painful memories with the earliest ones. When you think about what you shared with me in the last session, where would you like to begin? What could be the earliest memory that still bothers you?

Armando: We lived in one house until I was eleven, and then we moved to another place. In our house there was a bar, and on weekends… I remember the scenes of yelling and screaming because of my dad's drinking. I don't remember much at all before I was ten. My father always had dinner in a certain restaurant on Saturday evenings and would come home drunk. That is why there were so many arguments when he got home. There were many of these situations after I was eleven. I can't identify the reason for the fights and arguments my dad had with my mom. But I would often wind up getting in front of my mom because he would threaten to slap her.

One time the situation got really bad. My mother even called my paternal grandmother because my father was really losing it. There was so much confusion. That left a mark on me.

Another time...I do a lot of sports and there was a competition in the capital. We took longer to get home because there was a strong storm. We lived in a faraway part of town and we were late getting back. My father was waiting for us with a big club in his hand.

My mother just said: *"The neighbors are watching. What will they think?"*

On Sundays, he didn't drink because he had to recover from the hangovers so he could work on Mondays. When we would come home, we always had to speak quietly. I also remember at twilight on Saturdays…I would be watching TV with this horrible feeling that he would come home drunk. It was horrible anxiety. I would think: *he's going to come back soon and something is going to happen.* I would really get anxious about it. I also remember when I would carry him to bed because he was so drunk. I did that many times.

Once, my mother said she was going to leave home. She picked up the other kids, but I said I was going to stay with my dad. She wound up staying because of that. I felt sorry for my dad.

T: Of these old scenes, where do you think we could start?

A: I think the one with my dad holding the big club, waiting for us to get home. I remember the entrance to the building. We called the elevator and he was waiting for us with his arm raised! The gatekeeper was speechless. He didn't know what to do. In the end, we all just entered the elevator.

T: When you think about this experience, what are some of the negative words about yourself that feel false and irrational?

A: I need to do something and I don't know what.

T: What are the feelings that come up for you when you think about this?

A: Fear, anxiety, and shame.

T: On a scale of zero to ten, where ten is the maximum disturbance you can imagine and zero is none, how disturbing is it for you to think about that now?

A: Now? Almost nothing, but at the time, it was about a nine.

T: Where do you feel that in your body?

A: In my stomach.

T: Armando, we're going to start some bilateral movements (BLM) now. You can ask me to stop whenever you like, if necessary. I'm going to ask you to think about all of this, we'll do some movements in silence, and then we'll talk about it, okay?

A: That's fine.

T: So, think about this difficult experience that you described to me, think about the negative words, *I need to do something and I don't know what,* feel this in your body, and follow the movements. [The therapist was using a light bar to do the visual movements.]

[BLM.]

T: Take a deep breath. What comes up now?

A: Some feelings came up for me. I have to protect my mother. I need to keep people from getting hurt. I have an enormous feeling of injustice. The reason we were late was because of the rain. I really didn't know what to do. The person who was supposed to help me was the cause of the problem.

[BLM.]

T: And now?

A: Other scenes came up, other feelings…the problems would always start when evening began. These moments were pure torture. I would count the minutes until that was over. Until my dad went to sleep, the anxiety was enormous, the anxiety and the sense of danger.

[BLM.]

A: The anxiety came back. I would imagine him going to bed soon so that dangerous situation would finally end. I had very sharp ears that would pick up any sign that stuff was beginning to happen so I could intervene. Other scenes came up too.

I was on the football team. My dad never came to see me. I must have been about twelve years old and I was a really good player. I was the captain of the team, but he never came because on Saturdays he drank. I even became the national champion in another sport and he only came to the very last competition. But we were always afraid that he was going to pull a fast one on us.

[BLM].

Now another feeling came up. I won most of my competitions. I had the highest score when I went up to the podiums. He was never there. I wanted him to see me in that place of honor, where I received a prize for my talent. It made me sad. Instead I thought, *Now I need to go home because something bad may be happening there*. It was a strong feeling…that he never attended any of these important moments where I was so successful. He taught me to have such passion for his football team. It was the passion of doing things together with my dad. I always put the blame on the alcohol. It was stealing my father. I have memories of him during the week when he wouldn't drink and he would sometimes take me to work with him. I really liked that. During the week he was a normal father. That was very nice.

T: So tell this little boy that he doesn't live there anymore. Tell him something like, "Now you can live with me. The danger is over."

[BLM].

A: Is it okay to cry? My feelings say: *You made it! You were able to overcome this*! [Armando cries.] It's over. I miss what my father didn't teach me. I needed his wisdom and advice.

[BLM].

I'm okay now…just a bit emotional still.

Since it was almost time to end the session, and Armando had reached a good stopping point, the therapist began to wrap things up. She informed him about how the reprocessing could continue after the session and that he might remember other things as well. He might have dreams, or other feelings might come up, and he should feel free to get in touch if he needed to do so.

Identifying the Ruptures

It is very important to be able to identify where the breaks and ruptures have occurred because that is where the traumas live. This is where the adverse experiences of our lives hide and those will become the targets of therapeutic treatment. When we take our clients' history, we need to pay special attention to where life has broken. Often when we mention these experiences to our clients, they will say, "Oh, I'm over that. It's done." So I reply, "Let's make sure," and put it on the list of targets that I am compiling as we structure the treatment plan. If it is really resolved, we will zip through it during the reprocessing phase. But if it still needs fixing, reprocessing will clean out those painful networks.

During these first sessions, it was clear how much Armando's father's suicide weighed on him. There was still a lot that needed to be worked through in his relationship with his dad. But that wasn't the only thing. That first targeted memory of the elevator scene left its mark. Many people think that because something happened long ago, that it's over, or that they are able to deal with the memory in a way that it doesn't bother them as much. What we hear as Armando's story unfolds is how these ruptures, these breaks, still affected his life.

The issue of anxiety appears and reappears in his life and it is one of the things that keeps him from achieving his goals. A lot of people who come out of alcoholic homes struggle with anxiety. The unpredictability generates this sense of danger, which easily lends itself to a sense of anxiety. *What's going to happen today? How will my dad come home tonight?* Not knowing if the "nice dad" or the "bad dad" will arrive significantly complicated Armando's life, as it does in the majority of alcoholic homes.

Sometimes patients will come in with a presenting issue and think it's strange that we ask them about their past experiences. But if we don't get to the root of the past, it will be very difficult to resolve the situation in the present. There are parts of our brain that are activated with tragic circumstances—like Armando's dad's suicide. Time doesn't make it better because time doesn't reprocess frozen memories.

What EMDR therapy does is give the brain a second chance to digest these memories. This allows the brain to resolve several aspects of the anxiety-driven memories. The client loses the sense of being in constant danger, something that is characteristic of this condition. Resolving the anxiety in the past alleviates present-day experiences. It is a natural response or consequence. Later in Armando's story, we will see how the anxiety connected to public performance decreased to the point that Armando was able to acknowledge that he didn't have to do things perfectly. This freed him to accomplish things in a more relaxed way.

Reprocessing

Third session:

Once again, Armando and the therapist exchanged greetings, and she asked him how things were going.

Armando: I was fine when I left here last week, but then I spent a few days feeling kind of gloomy and introspective. The doctor made a few changes to my medication because of my anxiety level. Remembering all of those things…it was difficult to find myself in all of that. But it's over. I'm the one who controls these things now.

Armando talks about some other memories about that time in his life. He said that he didn't have any pertinent dreams about what we had worked on together that he could remember.

Therapist: Now when you think about the experience we worked on in the last session, what is it like?

A: It's fine. I see the scene, but I don't feel fear or terror. I see it as a difficult thing, but it is over. I don't know if this is temporary, but I see it as a picture. I overcame it. I survived and so did my mom.

The therapist asks about the present level of disturbance on a scale of zero to ten when Armando thinks about that scene, and Armando replies that it is zero.

We move on to the next disturbing scene that occurred around that time: his father's suicide.

A: When I remember my father's suicide, I think of two distinct moments. First, there was the moment when we received the news. I was the last person that had contact with him before he died. He said to me, "*I'm going for a little walk in the park.*" I found his note to my mother and I thought he had left home.

Later, there was all this hustle and bustle going on at my house, but I didn't have any idea what was going on. Our maid was the one who happened to meet the person who knew what had transpired, so she gave us the news. I felt so lost in the midst of all of that. My father had a gun, but my mother had given it away because of all of the problems they faced. A few days before all of this happened, there was a telephone call saying that the "order" had arrived. Later, we realized he had purchased another gun. I sat on the floor in the hallway and a neighbor stayed with me. It was twilight.

T: When you think about that scene, this difficult experience, what do you think about yourself that is false, negative, or irrational?

A: I'm lost.

T: What emotions come up when you think about all of this?

A: Anguish. When I see that note on the desk I feel terrible anguish.

T: On a scale of zero to ten, how much disturbance do you feel now when you think about that?

A: Six.

T: Where do you feel that in your body?

A: In my stomach.

T: Think about this difficult experience, the picture of the note on the desk, and think about the words, *I'm lost*. Feel that in your body and follow the movements.

[BLM].

A: I feel the anxiety that I felt at that moment. When my mother saw the note, she immediately thought of suicide. My dad had gone to his mother's house with a bag in his hand. Then he went to the park. That's where I think I failed. I wasn't able to help. I could have stopped him somehow. I should have done something to keep him from doing that.

[BLM].

A: It took a long time to find my feelings after that. I just consumed myself. I see it as a scene that doesn't fit. I don't question it.

I also remembered the phone call. I could have done something.

T: How could you have known that your father was planning to do this?

A: Yeah, I know…but I keep thinking that I should have done something.

[BLM].

T: Armando, it seems that there are two "Armandos" here: one that keeps saying that he needed to do something to keep his father from doing what he did, and the other one that knows that maybe there wasn't really a whole lot that could have been done. Maybe these two "Armandos" can talk to each other. Perhaps you, the Adult, could explain to this young man what happened.

[BLM].

A: It took a bit of doing, but I was able to talk to them a little bit.

T: It seems that your dad carefully thought through this decision. It was well prepared. He left a note. He bought a gun he kept hidden from everyone else. He chose a form of death that wouldn't give him much of a chance to survive. It seems he was resolute about doing this. I think it was simply a matter of time. If it hadn't been that day, it would have been another. Maybe there was nothing that could have been done to keep him from going through with it. Maybe you could explain this to the Armando that keeps insisting that he should have done something?

[BLM].

A: I remembered something else, a sense of guilt. This was after I found out about his psychiatric diagnosis. I didn't know about that. But I was just an adolescent!

[BLM].

T: Now, when you think about this difficult experience, how much disturbance do you feel?

A: With regard to finding the note, I'm more relieved. It bothers me just a little bit, a zero or a one. I will continue working on the guilt. But everything is clearer, more in focus. It's better now.

The other scene I remembered was the funeral. This was really painful. When I went back to school, I remembered how embarrassed and ashamed I was. People were commenting, "*It was his father who committed suicide.*" Everyone knew it and I was so ashamed.

T: All of this is really difficult and very painful. Our time is ending today, so maybe we can take this up at our next session? Is that all right?

A: Yes. There are a lot of memories, but I am more relieved.

Repair

Fourth session

Therapist: So, Armando, how are you doing?

A: Pretty good. I did better this week. I didn't feel anything. I didn't have the emotional hangover I had the other time. I wasn't anxious about coming to session today.

T: Now when you think about the experience that we worked on last week, what is it like?

A: It's fine. It's like something that happened to me, left its mark, disrupted the rhythm of my life, but I understand I really couldn't do anything. The note still brings up a bit of anxiety. When I think about opening the drawer and seeing the note…that's not good.

T: How much disturbance do you feel when you think about this?

A: Three.

T: So, think about this difficult experience, the one with the note, and follow the movements.

[BLM].

A: I get a feeling of nostalgia, of homesickness, of longing. It was a watershed moment in my life. I wish it hadn't happened, but it's not my fault. It's okay. Whether or not there was a note, I couldn't have done anything differently. I just miss him.

T: How much disturbance do you feel when you think about this now?

A: One. Maybe two. It doesn't bother me. There's not that same impact anymore. Now I just miss him. There was a rupture, a break, a loss.

When all of this happened, we all stayed home. A friend of mine came over. I went to sleep at my aunt's house because we were close. I was just trying to process what had happened, understand it, gather information. I didn't know how to react, how to make it better. The next day, I knew that I wanted to go to the funeral, but my siblings didn't go.

T: In this part of the experience, what scene or photograph stands out for you?

A: Me, sitting in the hallway with my friend…feeling empty, lost, and trying to understand the situation.

T: When you think about this scene, what are the negative, false, or irrational words that you think about yourself?

A: I'm lost. I don't know how to handle this situation. Where this is going?

T: What emotions come up for you when you think about this?

A: Anxiety, confusion.

T: How much disturbance do you feel?

A: Three. I feel some sad nostalgia, but there was another component. I was in a place where I was surrounded by other people, and that bothered me. I didn't want to show weakness. I had to be strong.

T: Where do you feel that in your body?

A: In my stomach.

T: So think about all of this, these negative words, and follow the movements.

[BLM].

A: The pain is gone, as well as the sense of shame. I had this excessive concern with what others would think, because of all of the turmoil and the embarrassing, alcoholic scenes my father would make. On top of that, the shame of him killing himself. Shame. I don't have any more shame about that now, but I did for years. A lot of shame. I would tell others it had been an accident. But today it's okay. The shame was back then. The image had been frozen. Now I recognize those feelings and they don't bother me anymore.

[BLM].

A: Today I have heartburn. I feel a lot of things in my stomach. But I'm good about that scene. It's a zero.

The next scene was at my aunt's house. There was a lot of confusion going on. I turned out the light and looked up, thinking about what to do with my life.

I'm alone. At this point, there was a rupture with God. He couldn't exist. These things just couldn't happen. I was the oldest of my siblings.

[BLM].

Heavier than all of the confusion was the idea that I would never see him again. We would never have any more contact. That was very painful.

[BLM].

A: It's over. I survived. I was able to get past that moment. I didn't turn to drugs or alcohol. I absorbed the strong principles of integrity and honesty that came from my father. Life moved forward.

[BLM].

A: Not just me, but my whole family survived that situation. No one froze. My mother survived. Eventually, she even found someone else. It's okay. Things are okay.

T: Let's look at the scene of the funeral? We still have time today.

A: The funeral was easier. There I was, arriving at the cemetery…what an ugly scene. The chapel is made of marble; everything was gray, made of concrete. I arrived and saw the coffin. Something important happened. There was this guy at the funeral who wound up teaching us all a lesson. He was the son of the owner of the bar where my dad was a frequent customer. My dad would drink at home, but sometimes he would go to the bar down the street. I had met the owner's children. When this fellow arrived, I broke down into tears. A friend took me aside and we went to get a cold drink.

[BLM].

I had the sudden feeling of despair, but now the disturbance is almost nothing; zero.

A: Since we began working on all of this stuff, the anxiety has not come back. However, I feel a certain wistfulness, a longing for my dad. With regard to the rupture, I'm fine. The scene of my friend taking me outside was also very important. But to carry the coffin; see it that close…it was a moment of total despair.

T: You know, Armando, when someone suddenly dies like this, we don't have a chance to say goodbye. A lot of things are left unsaid, including important things that we wish they knew before they left. I would like to suggest an exercise. Imagine that your dad can come here from wherever he is and you get a chance to tell him everything that you needed to say: how important he was to you, how much you missed him growing up, and anything else you felt wasn't expressed. Tell him whatever you want. You can do that here. Think about all of that and follow the movements.

[BLM].

[Armando cries as he goes through his farewell to his dad.] I thanked him for all of the wonderful values he passed on to me. There really wasn't any way I could help him. I was just an adolescent. Every person has his own rationale for what he does. I don't have to judge him. I don't hate him. He had his reasons. He struggled until there was a moment when he just couldn't keep going. I thanked him for having left us in a good place, financially. It was one of his concerns.

T: All right. Now let's listen to what he wants to say to you...

[BLM].

A: Two things: he asked me for forgiveness, to forgive him for what he did, and he congratulated me for having helped the family follow a good path.

Both of us were very moved. We shared our final comments and said goodbye. It was a very emotional session, but one of enormous repair.

Making Peace with Our Past

One of the therapeutic tasks that usually comes up in therapy is repair: making our peace with the past. But for this to happen, sometimes it is necessary to make peace with what actually happened and with whoever was in the experience. Accepting what happened does not mean condoning it. Acceptance means saying, *"Things are the way they are, and they happened the way they did."* We can't change the past, but we can change our perception and our interpretation of what we remember.

In this case, Armando suddenly lost his dad, in a violent and unexpected way. There wasn't an opportunity to personally say goodbye, since his father was gone by the time Armando found out about it.

One of the clinical strategies we can use is repair. My first training was in Psychodrama, and I often borrow ideas from that approach. We can use what is called Internal Psychodrama, which allows us to process what is happening in the patient's imagination while they have internal dialogues or interweaving discussions. This allows for possibilities in resolution during processing.

One of the issues that comes up as we deal with trauma is unfinished business, or the unfinished step. The feeling is that something was left hanging. Some people repeatedly put themselves into vulnerable and high-risk situations in an unconscious attempt to bring closure to traumatic circumstances they have experienced. Since our brains "ask" for an ending (for resolution), and preferably a happy one, an Internal Psychodrama fulfills this need very well.

In the session, there was time to give Armando's situation an appropriate ending. That is where the idea of having Armando speak to his dad originated. It was a way of helping him bring closure to his father's death, since this was such an important relationship in his life. So we had him imagine that his father came to speak with him, and gave Armando an opportunity to have a private conversation, in his own thoughts, while processing any regret to alleviate the pain of this great loss.

Maybe one of the best things about EMDR therapy is that it offers the patients a sense of protection and safety because they don't have to give the specific details of what happened in the experience they are processing. Armando said very little about what went on in their conversation, but he came out of it feeling much better. The important thing is that he had a chance to bring this relationship to a satisfactory resolution. There are moments that are so private—and sacred—that they should remain in the silence of our thoughts.

We also offered him a chance to let him hear what he imagined his father would say to him, words that were surprisingly positive and confirming. So there was ultimately a two-way resolution to the relationship.

Reconciliation

Fifth Session

The therapist asked Armando how things had gone since his last session.

Armando: That day I was pretty introspective, but the next day I was just fine.

Therapist: When you think about that experience now, how much does it bother you from zero to ten?

A: Zero.

T: Okay, let's move on to the next experience on our list. It has to do with having gone to boarding school.

A: Yes. I went to a military school. I was able to pass the rigorous entrance exams. My father passed away in May and I went away to school the following February. I had a commander that was very exacting and I wasn't able to go home much on the weekends. It was very much like a military regime at school. I had to call home from a public phone back then. Often, the call wouldn't go through or would cut out while I was talking to my mother. It was really complicated.

When I think about this, several scenes come to mind: first, is the trip to boarding school. When I took my entrance exams, I was refused entrance because of an eyesight problem. However, I won my appeal and was able to attend. All of us that had been approved were put on the same bus and taken to the boarding school many miles away. I was worried about what I was leaving behind. There were a lot of people on the bus and I've always been an introvert. It was a tough trip. When I got to the school, I realized it was a really big place.

I was very proud of myself because only 200 of the 100,000 candidates had passed. But I had to come to terms with the fact that I was leaving home forever and I was only fifteen. I thought, *Wow, I don't have my father's support.*

T: What are the words that best describe you when you think about this scene that are negative, false, or irrational

A: *I don't have any support.* I'm leaving my siblings behind.

T: When you think about this, what emotions come up for you?

A: Sadness.

T: On a scale of zero to ten, where ten is the greatest disturbance and zero is none, how much disturbance do you feel when you think about this?

A: Six. That thing about going onto the bus…with all of these people I didn't know. I wasn't afraid of much after my dad died. Not being afraid helped strengthen me, but that day I was concerned with what I was going to have to face.

T: Where do you feel that in your body?

A: In my stomach; an emptiness. I have a real emptiness. I don't know what to do with those emotions. It could have been different. It was an emptiness due to the circumstances.

[BLM].

T: What could have helped you?

A: Knowing that my family was going to be just fine. That would have helped me.

T: So, in your imagination, please tell Teenage Armando what you know today; that your family did just fine without him.

[BLM].

A: Teenage Armando is good. It was so complicated to call home. It was expensive. I could imagine what my mom was going through. She was wise. She didn't let me leave school after the first year when I wanted to. She made me stay.

T: So let's thank your mom?

[BLM].

A: I have much to be grateful for. She never showed weakness. Sometimes I would go a whole month without going home. Sometimes she would come to visit me. She was a safe harbor. I always send her special greetings on Father's Day.

T: So when you go back and think about boarding the bus, how much disturbance do you feel, from zero to ten?

A: One. It's mostly anxiety and a concern about them.

A scene that stayed in my mind was arriving at the boarding school. There were several wings to the school, and closets with beds underneath. We were all talking at the door, without really knowing what we were supposed to do or what to expect.

Now when I think about that first day, I'm fine. I came to understand that those folks were partners. I was kind of popular because I was an athlete. There were competitions. There was a lot of hazing but I wound up winning over the older guys, even that first year.

One time, a bunch of us pulled a fast one and got into trouble, but I really never had discipline problems. Sometimes I would provoke some of the guys from the second year, just to show off, but it wasn't a big deal.

T: So, now when you think about this experience, how much does it bother you from zero to ten?

A: Arriving at school? Zero.

The truth is that I have a lot of good memories, just wonderful experiences there. Sometimes I felt like I was losing my life in there. I was really being prepared for a military career and I would think, *I am never going to use this.* My country will never go to war with anyone, so it had no meaning.

I would think, *I'm losing years of my life in here.* I thought of several scenes that made a particular impression. Once, I went home to visit. I would get home really late sometimes and then go back to school Sunday night. I would get very sad with that whole routine. My sister was going to parties and there I was going back to boarding school!

But it's over. I left the school. I went down a different path. I overcame in other ways. The sadness became learning. It stayed back there as well. I worked hard. I finished high school way ahead of everyone else. I came in thirteenth place in the college entrance exams for the federal university.

[BLM].

When all is said and done, I didn't finish military school. I did a year and eight months. Before I finished the second year, I went back to my old school, where my family lived. I finished my last year there. This time, my mother let me come home.

The last day that I was at boarding school, we had an exercise where we had to sleep out in the open. These were experiences that strengthened my character. I learned loyalty and honesty. I think I am more loyal than honest. I believe in fulfilling your duty…and faithfulness. All of these things became deeply ingrained in my character.

I had a couple of pretty serious hazing experiences. Once I got kicked by an officer and couldn't respond. Sometimes they worked us out so brutally that the next day I could hardly climb the stairs.

[BLM].

Military school was a learning experience in my life. I felt a lot of sadness, but everything is all right now. It's good; resolved. One grows up, and cultivates different things. I cultivated many things for many years. After I came into contact with the Bible I really changed. Before, I seemed to enjoy my suffering. That changed after my conversion. Now things are good. It's part of my past experience. It was a time of learning.

Today, we had a meeting at work with a lot of important people. My boss was supposed to be there, but an important person from our team passed away, one of our friends. He had a car accident. So I woke up that morning and I knew I was going to have to substitute for my boss at the meeting. I thought, *I'm going to have to sit next to one of those politicians who is always trying to boycott our work.*

When these thoughts surfaced, I remembered my sister's death for some reason. I was the marrow donor in an attempt to save her life, but it didn't work out. That bothers me.

T: Okay. I think that's a whole new theme that we can work on in our next session. You were not responsible for healing your sister. You did the best you could. Things don't always turn out the way we want them to.

A: That's right. Let's work on this in the next session.

Sixth session

Armando: I'm doing well. I wake up a bit more tired. But I'm in a good mood. I have days that are really full and stressful. I've woken up more anxious, and sometimes startled, but I am able to stabilize almost immediately.

Therapist: I'd like you to think about what we worked on last session. How much disturbance do you feel, on a scale of zero to ten?

A: It doesn't bother me anymore. It's zero. They were situations that happened within their context. It was just part of the school of life. What remains today is good. The bad stuff got left behind in those moments.

My sister's death was something that I went through from far away because I had already left home. I believed that the Lord would heal her. I had hoped for a miracle when there was nothing more that could be done. She died under the eyes of the Lord, something that consoles me very much. I was a real pill of a brother. I could have been more loving. I wish we had had more time together. But I take comfort in the fact that I was the donor. The week before I was scheduled to go to the hospital, I was in a terrible nervous state. She died young, but fought the cancer for many years.

There is another scene that I remembered where they baptized my brother's son. My sister made a real point of going to that, but she was already struggling to breathe. The day she died she went to the hospital. It was God's intervention that allowed us to even find a bed for her there. I went with my brother-in-law to their town so we could tell my mother. I only saw her the next day, at the funeral. I wish I had been a better brother. I think she carried some emotional scars because of my behavior. But my brother-in-law always said my sister had enormous admiration for me.

I remember how I would pick on her when we were young. I once broke an egg on her head. We were just playing around. Another time, when I left military school, I chose to be in her classroom. She cried because I wanted to be there. She was a year behind me, and I kept telling her she was ugly. But she was beautiful!

T: Which of these scenes do you want to start with?

A: The one where I broke the egg on her head.

T: So, when you think about this difficult experience, what do you think about yourself that is false, negative, or irrational?

A: I'm bad. I'm insensitive.

T: What emotions come up for you when you think about all of this?

A: Enormous regret. I wish I could go back and change these moments.

T: On a scale of zero to ten, where ten is the greatest disturbance, how much disturbance do you feel when you think about all of this?

A: Seven. I want to go back and do things differently.

T: Where do you feel that in your body?

A: On my shoulders; in my heart.

T: Okay, Armando. Think about this scene and the words, *I'm bad*. Feel these things in your body and follow the movements.

[BLM].

A: Other scenes came up where I said she was dumb, but she was very smart. She just needed to study more. Picking on her was my way of showing her I loved her. We didn't learn how to properly show love at home.

T: Armando, once again, I would like to give you the opportunity to have a conversation with your sister. Imagine that she comes here and the two of you have a chance to talk. Tell her the things that you wish you could have said to her. How about it?

A: Let's do it.

[BLM]. [Armando cries during the eye movements.]

I am very comforted with her response. She knew that it was just kids' stuff. But even so, it wasn't a nice thing to do.

[BLM].

A: I said to the Armando on the inside who keeps lamenting that he can't go back to the past, that there really is no way to go back. My sister understood the circumstances. I then talked to the Ever-Lamenting Armando and told him there is no way to go back. She knew his feelings for her, how much young Armando loved her, and she understood.

T: So, perhaps now you can imagine a future where you can replace what didn't happen?

[BLM].

A: It is very comforting to know that I will be able to love with transparency.

T: When you think about this experience, how much disturbance do you feel?

A: Zero.

My sister's illness had an excellent prognosis for healing. The treatment was simple, but I saw that it wasn't quite like that. She was treated in the best hospitals with the best doctors. I went with her to an appointment. It deeply impacted me to walk in that wing where people were waiting—people who had this disease—and others who were already in treatment. Waiting was pure anguish. I saw children with cancer and their suffering mothers. Another tough moment was the day after her transplant.

T: So, think about these scenes in the hospital.

[BLM].

A: Several things came up…like the moment when we did the exams and it became clear that I would be the donor. I had a certain feeling of anxiety, a fear of the procedure, but also the satisfaction of being able to help. I had absolute conviction that God would heal her, and I felt an enormous responsibility, when I was doing the prep work, to properly prepare for the transplant.

T: When you think about this, how much does it bother you now, from zero to ten?

A: Three. I was listening to the instructions during the appointment and taking the meds they prescribed. They gave me an injection to increase the production of stem cells.

[BLM].

I took the meds and got a headache, plus some crazy anxiety. I felt like my body had to be perfect. I had to be the rescuer in this situation. I was also afraid of having a panic attack again. I didn't sleep right. My wife came to stay with me. A childhood teacher came as well. As a matter of fact, she was the one who took me aside, and said, *"You are not responsible for curing your sister, okay?"*

[BLM].

Now I only have immense gratitude to the Lord for how things went. This teacher identified my anguish. Now all the scenes are calm.

T: On a scale of zero to ten, how is it now?

A: Zero.

The week of the transplant—when they did the infusion for my sister—I did everything I was supposed to do: I got the shots, I was very careful about what I ate, etc. They could have even done more infusions. Everything went really well. It was comforting to know that I did my part. I thought, *Okay, now she's going to be healed.*

T: When you think about this difficult experience, how much is the disturbance?

A: Zero.

A really neat scene came up. There was a time when she could barely breathe. I went to spend a week with her, just the two of us, spending time together. Later, an aunt said that she had really appreciated my visit. There hadn't been any problems. She said, *"When my brother is here, the whole place lights up!"*

T: Think about these positive words, *I did the best I could*. On a scale of one to seven, where seven is completely true and one is completely false, how true do you feel these words are now, thinking about that experience with your sister?

A: Seven. My feelings of regret have been adjusted. There's no disturbance. I'm at peace with all of this.

Making Peace with the Folks Who Live Inside

In this session, we saw that Armando still carried feelings of regret regarding the loss of his sister. This is a very common response when one loses someone in this fashion. Since he was the donor for his sister's transplant, it's very easy to connect the dots that think, *I'm the one who can save her.* This teacher's comforting words were providential, helping Armando understand that he was not responsible for his sister's life or her death, for that matter.

We also saw how Armando was coming to terms and making peace with the situation of his father, and how that's continuing to strengthen with each session. This inner reconciliation was important because it brought him peace and resolution.

It was freeing for him to understand that he had given his best to his sister. It dispelled the feelings of guilt and the sense of responsibility for her death. He felt something similar with regard to his father, although in another dimension. But in both instances, he felt that he hadn't done enough to save their lives. Both deaths had an enormous impact on his life, in different ways, and just needed to be stored in the proper files of his past.

Another role that Armando needed to work through was that of the teenager who had gone to boarding school. All of us have "folks who live inside," different roles that develop inside of us.[6] Sometimes they take over control of our adult life, which is not an appropriate function for these roles. In this particular

---

[6] The author has a book by that name, *Healing the Folks Who Live Inside.*

case, it was important for Armando to acknowledge the adolescent who left home and to let him know that everything worked out well. Sometimes our inner roles don't know how the story ended, and through the use of these internal dialogues, it is possible to inform them. One of the important therapeutic tasks is the integration or reconciliation of the inner gallery of roles. This teenager didn't know how the story ended, so it was important that Armando let him know.

Finally, Armando was also able to recognize the importance of his mother's role in his life. Gratitude is an emotion of enormous healing and is a sign that important changes for the better are taking place. Armando was able to even thank his father for the values that he had given him while growing up.

Resolution

Seventh session

Therapist: So, Armando, how was your week? We worked on a lot of difficult issues last time.

Armando: Yes, we did, but I really feel *that I did what I could.* God gave me the blessing of being able to be my sister's donor. She gained more time.

T: When you think about what we worked on last week, how much disturbance do you feel now?

A: None. No disturbance at all.

I think it is time to begin working on what initially brought me here. When I think about doing a public presentation, I lose my breath and my voice breaks up. I get scared about what is going to happen, so it happens. I was always shy. I was an easy-going child. I was always playing with my toys. I was never hyper.

But I have always had a need for approval I wanted to say the right thing, have the most intelligent presentations, etc. I work in an environment with people I really admire. It's a calm place, but I have to demonstrate my abilities. That's where the anxiety and the panic come into the picture.

T: Can you picture a clear scene where these kinds of things happen?

A: Yes. I remember when I had to go to two presentations, in a really large auditorium. It was totally full. There were a lot of important people there. My boss was supposed to go, but at the last minute, something came up and I had to go in his place. I was the last one to speak, hoping that my boss might show up. I had my speech ready. When it was my turn to speak, I kept thinking that I was not going to make it, and that I would stutter, lose my breath, or freeze.

Then it was my turn to speak. My colleague said his part and I said mine.

T: When you think about this situation, what do you think about yourself that is negative?

A: I'm a coward.

T: What emotions come up for you?

A: Fear. Anxiety.

T: On a scale of zero to ten, how much disturbance do you feel when you think about this?

A: Seven.

T: Where do you feel that in your body?

A: I get this feeling of anxiety in my stomach and it presses on my lungs.

T: So think about this experience, think about the words, *I'm a coward,* feel this in your body, and follow the movements.

[BLM].

A: I can't feel a sensation. I remembered other facts that happened. A few years ago, I called the phone company to make a complaint and I lost my breath. The same thing happened when I called a restaurant for home delivery.

[BLM]

A: There were a lot of moments from the past, but I wasn't able to specifically identify anything. At home, there was a lot of pressure. My father made it clear that he expected me to be the best. My mother also required a lot from me. I was one of the best students. I had to show up and do well.

[BLM].

A: I've always been critical with others as well. I think that other people may be thinking the same thing about me.

In another situation, there was a championship at the boarding school when I was young. I was never able to reach the level I'd hoped to achieve. They only let me compete in the second round.

T: How much disturbance do you feel when you think about this?

A: Seven. I think I didn't do as well as I could have.

[BLM].

A: Another situation came up. I was really good at sports, but I was very skinny. I think that if I had given more of myself, I could have gone to the championship, and even competed for the national title. It bothers me that I didn't work harder.

[BLM].

A: There's a scene when I was 12 years old. I was at a high level in my sport. I liked other sports as well, but training for them was easy for me. I had natural talent, but I wouldn't finish practice. Even so, I won numerous championships. I even beat my greatest rival. Two years later, he was the state champion. He really developed a lot.

[BLM].

A: The world is very competitive. I thought training and practice were boring. Then I would think, *I can't fail; I have to be the best or others will criticize me.*

[BLM].

A: A bunch of thoughts came up. I went through a period where I was really a "bum." I had just graduated. I had income from a rental. The people who studied with me in college and admired me began to study harder. They started getting really good jobs. I was just kind of halfway studying. I didn't take my exams seriously. Some people had parents who would support them for years so they could pass difficult exams and get high-paying government jobs, but I needed to dedicate myself more.

In the end, life took a lucky turn. I ran into the young lady who today is my wife. I went into private business. Later, I lost my job because of political issues, so I really began to seriously study. I lost my job, even though I was the best regional manager of my firm at the time. Some public government positions opened. That was what I really wanted.

T: Well, our time today is coming to an end. How do you feel now?

A: I'm fine. I just have a lot of things to think about…

Eighth session

I'm doing well. I'm doing really well at my events. I have more confidence to face the situations at work.

T: When you think about the things that we worked on in our last session, how much do they bother you now?

A: Now it's a three. In the end, everything turned out all right. It bothers me that I spent so much time in a frozen state. But it's in the past. Still, I wish I had done better.

T: What can you think about yourself that you'd like to be positive?

A: I can make mistakes. I don't have to be perfect.

T: On a scale of one to seven, where seven is completely true, how true do you feel these words are now when you think about that?

A: Two. I can't make mistakes. I have to be perfect.

T: When you think about these negative words, what emotions come up for you?

A: Anguish.

T: On a scale of zero to ten?

A: Three.

T: Where do you feel that in your body?

A: In my stomach.

T: So, think about that scene from last week, and think about the words, *I have to be perfect. I can't make mistakes*. Feel that in your body, and follow the movements.

[BLM].

A: I remembered two situations. One happened last Saturday. I was in a place full of important people. It gave me a lot of anxiety, at first. I got a lot of compliments on my speech, but the microphone bothered me a lot.

In the end, everything turned out all right; everything changed, like it was just transformed. It was worthy of note. Later, in another situation, I maintained a very confident stance.

Yesterday, I was in a meeting full of VIPs, but I was at ease. I also had to use a microphone there. I felt like if they gave me the microphone that I would do just fine. I could see how to bring together all of my ideas.

But my fear of freezing up or failing is complicated.

[BLM].

A: You know something? Who cares? I can freeze, fail, and make mistakes! The solution is to just take a deep breath and ask to speak later on so that I can use the gift that I have in the best possible way.

T: Okay, go back to the initial scene that gave you all of that adrenaline.

A: I usually start by greeting everyone who is present.

[BLM].

A: I am overcoming it. The feeling is going away.

T: Maybe you can see the greeting as a warm-up?

A: Yes.

[BLM].

T: Perhaps you can view the microphone as your friend? After all, it's the microphone that makes it possible for people to hear the well-formulated ideas you have.

[BLM].

A: The microphone is an instrument that helps me develop the talent God gave me. It is not a bad thing. It is my helper.

T: Exactly. Now, think about the words, *I can use the microphone well*. On a scale of one to seven, where seven is completely true, how true does it feel to you now?

A: Six.

[BLM].

A: Now it's seven.

T: A powerful seven?

A: Yes.

T: Let's check something. When you think about the words, *I'm going to freeze up,* how much disturbance do you feel, from zero to ten?

A: Zero. I might freeze up but it's okay.

[BLM].

A: I feel really grounded.

T: When you think about the next time you'll have to face situations where you have to speak in public, what's it like?

A: It is going to be a total success!

[BLM].

A: I'm good.

T: Now imagine some problems surfacing.

[BLM].

A: If something happens…well, it's just part of life. I will figure it out. Things will fall into place.

T: If you go blank?

A: I'll just tell the audience and start over.

T: When you think about all of this and the anxiety, how much disturbance do you feel?

A: Zero. Sunday I will have to give an interview at the local radio station. That will be the test.

T: Okay, so imagine yourself doing this interview.

[BLM].

A: Since this is an unusual situation, and I rarely give radio interviews, it gives me butterflies in my stomach. I'm well prepared, but my stomach feels it.

[BLM].

T: Now?

A: One.

[BLM].

A: Now it's zero. I can do it. I can see myself doing it without any stress.

Ninth (and Last) Session

Armando: I'm doing really well. I think I'm ready to end therapy. I went through some experiences with the microphone and it didn't faze me one bit. I did everything with all the serenity in the world. I went to the radio station. I was able to easily ad lib. I did a presentation without any anxiety or worries.

Therapist: So, let's evaluate your therapy goals. When you first arrived, we put together a treatment plan and set up some targets we felt we needed to work on. Let's go through them now and see how we have done.

A: Sounds great.

T: One of your goals was to feel more at ease with yourself. When you think about this now, on a scale of zero to ten, where ten is completely resolved and zero is not resolved at all, how much do you feel this goal has been reached?

A: Ten. I think I was even able to remove the weight of the anxiety and the fear. I don't respond like that anymore. I can do things calmly and naturally, like a daily routine.

T: Another issue was the fact that you grew up in an alcoholic home and were affected by all of the complications that entails. On that same scale, how resolved do you think that is now?

A: Also a ten. It's done.

T: Your father's suicide?

A: Ten. You know, it was really good to work on that. I had never done it before. There was a time when I harbored the sadness, the fact that it made me suffer so much. It was really good to work on that because now I feel like it is completely resolved. Even the guilty feelings about when he left home that last time are gone. To be able to understand that it was premeditated and there really was nothing I could have done to help him felt like the release of a burden I'd been carrying for most of my life... At fifteen, there wasn't a lot that I could have done. I was the son that I should have been.

T: How about your sister's death?

A: Yeah…I was the donor. For a long time, I asked myself, "Why didn't the marrow work?" I was such a bully of a brother. We became really good friends when we grew up and then I lost those opportunities to further strengthen our bond. But I am dealing with that better now.

T: On a scale of zero to ten, how resolved do you feel that is now?

A: I still miss her. I would have liked to have had more experiences with her. But it is resolved. I think I just have a longing for her presence. But when I get to Heaven, that will be settled. So I would give it a nine, because I still miss her.

T: Another issue we worked on was the fact that you had to be perfect.

A: I think that can work as my compass, but I don't have to be rigid about it. There's room for mistakes and failures or forgetting something. You can't get away from that. At some point, we all makes mistakes, but I can live with that. I give it a ten.

T: How about the phobia at college and the panic attacks?

A: I really had a lot of fears and panic attacks during college. One night, I went to a nightclub with my friends and I had to go back home. Situations like that were common. I would go out by myself, things would come up, and I would have to leave. But I would be fine on the way home.

T: So what number would you give it on our scale?

A: It was a difficult time. Back then we didn't understand what was going on; these days we do. I couldn't understand what was happening to me at the time. But life has changed. I don't have a problem with that stuff anymore. I give it a ten: totally resolved.

I have really appreciated this whole therapeutic process...it's like magic! I really thought it was impossible to fix these things, and yet we did. It's not just what happens here in the session; during the week, it seems that things continue to get better and work themselves out. After that first session, I had some hard days when I felt really down. After the second session I had one difficult day, but from then on it wasn't hard at all. This kind of work continues over time. We hit the "start button" here and the process continues. But it really felt like magic. It's hard to believe. One has to go through it to feel it. The therapy process was so organized and there was so much empathy. That helped a lot.

T: It's been an incredible process, Armando. I have been very touched and moved to see how you have achieved your goals. It's just amazing.

We still have a few minutes left in our session, so I thought we could do something positive to end our process.

A: Sure thing.

T: I would like for you to think about the good experiences that you had in childhood. This exercise is called the Pillars of Life. It's when we go back and connect with those experiences that help build us. So go back to your childhood and think about the good things that happened to you and tell me the first good experience that you can remember.

A: I remember some of the presents that I got, some toys, and really nice birthday memories. My mother was excited about preparing a great birthday party. The cake always had something special on it and all of us helped.

There was a birthday cake that was a boat full of pirates! It started to melt, so it had to stay in front of the air conditioning until party time. That was really neat.

T: When you think about this experience, what do you think about yourself that is positive?

A: I can help…or even better: I am loved.

T: What positive emotions come up for you when you think about these positive words?

A: Love, affection, and joy.

T: Where do you feel that in your body?

A: In my chest.

T: So think about all of this and follow the movements. [Therapist does a few slow bilateral movements.]

A: Very nice.

A: It reminds me of my football team. We would buy birthday kits and put all of the items together for the party. I think I have a picture of this in one of my scrapbooks. It was a wonderful day. At this particular party, everyone had to come wearing the T-shirt of their favorite football team. My dad and I wore ours and we played ball in the yard. It was a very happy day, full of such enthusiasm and joy.

T: You said there were several memories. What's another one?

A: We all went out to dinner one Saturday evening. I remember that it was a place we went fairly often. I loved the spaghetti and meatballs. This restaurant still exists. When I go to my hometown, I still go there and ask for spaghetti and meatballs. Even though these things only happened on days that my dad was drinking, we still had a nice time.

T: So think about all of this and follow the movements. [Therapist does a few slow bilateral movements.]

A: I see a kind of consolidation of that feeling of us as a family, you know, everyone sitting around the table, eating at the same time. These Saturday evening dinners were very special, with all of us there together.

I remembered something else. My sister and I would lie in the back seat of the car and count the telephone poles as we drove past them. That was fun. My other siblings hadn't been born yet. It's a really pleasant memory. After so many poles, something was supposed to happen. It's nice to remember that time, especially since it was with my sister who passed away. You know, I was a good brother. During my adolescence, things changed, but at that time, we were just kids. My dad's drinking didn't get in the way.

T: So think about all of this and follow the movements. [Therapist does a few slow bilateral movements.]

A: I remembered another scene. I wanted a racetrack and a Falcon toy doll. These were expensive, and my day was pretty miserly. My mother's salary wasn't much and it was an expensive toy. My mother took me to the store to put it on layaway, and paid for it in a number of payments. I don't know how many. But she bought the racetrack.

The Falcon didn't come from my parents. It was imported from abroad. It was my father's friends who gave it to me. They arrived with the Falcon that I wanted so much. It was a soldier and I just loved it.

I even remember the scene with the racetrack…going into the store. The box was really heavy. The first few times I didn't even know how to deal with the accelerator!

It was a bit different with the Falcon, because it was a surprise. It came from other people. I had wanted it for a long time and it came out of an unexpected place.

T: When you think about these presents, what do you think about yourself that is positive?

A: I think about the love, the loyalty, and the companionship in the family. We siblings all slept in the same room until a certain age. I put the racetrack in an oval circuit in our room. I remember it to this day.

T: So think about all of this and follow the movements. [Therapist does a few slow bilateral movements.]

T: Well Armando, I just want to tell you how wonderful it has been working with you. It's been great to watch your progress and see how you have overcome so much. I want to congratulate you for such beautiful therapeutic work. It has been enlightening, significant, and fruitful. In fact, it's been so worthwhile that I would like to ask you for your permission to share it with others.

A: Oh, yes, of course. If this can help other people, I'm more than happy to authorize it.

T: Great. Armando, I see therapy a bit like going to the doctor. We have worked on some really important things that were getting in your way. Now you know how therapy works and that you respond well to this kind of treatment. I have your notes, so if anything ever surfaces, please come back and we can do a few sessions to clear it up, okay?

A: Yes, I will do that if I need it. Thank you for everything.

Ending

Here, we say goodbye to Armando and his story. Some final comments:

I developed this "ending scale" precisely to help evaluate the evolution of the treatment plan. It helps us see if the patient is ready to end therapy, although we know that the patient can stop at any time. But it is also useful for the client to see his or her own progress. In this case, Armando was able to express that he was genuinely ready to end therapy, since he had reached the goals that had brought him to therapy in the first place.

With clear goals, it is much easier to make a decision about whether to continue with therapy. It also helps structure the therapeutic process, since the treatment plan helps guide the way things unfold.

In this sense, we can see how EMDR therapy offers a wonderful paradigm for treating our clients. It is a different way of conducting therapy, since it uses the bilateral movements as part of the resolution of the clients' difficulties. It is possible to organize clear goals, a plan, concrete results, and undeniable scientific recognition.

We hope this study can illustrate how to organize the therapy process with clarity to help the client reach his or her goals. It also demonstrates how EMDR therapy can help repair the past—as well as relationships—to live a better life in the present. It allows people to look to a future of greater quality of life, make better choices, and to live a life of reconciliation with relationships that are truly satisfying.

That is our desire for your life as well.

About TraumaClinic do Brasil

The **TraumaClinic do Brasil** opened its doors in March 2014, initially as an expansion of the psychotherapy practice that Esly Regina Carvalho, Ph.D. was developing in Brasilia. However, as the number of people who needed treatment for their issues grew—many of which were linked to problems with traumas, anxiety, and depression—she felt the need to reach out to a greater number of people who struggle with these issues. She invited trusted colleagues to become team members. Using the new reprocessing approaches, especially EMDR therapy, the staff reaches out to people who have difficulties dealing with daily life and its challenges.

Our mission: help people overcome the challenges of life.

Our vision: offer high quality psychotherapy with excellence, ethics, and compassion so that we can help people overcome the challenges of life.

Our values: we are governed by the eternal values of integrity, honesty, transparency, and compassion toward all people.

Quality of treatment

Our clients' recovery is our highest priority. In an effort to maintain the highest level of quality treatment, the **TraumaClinic do Brasil** invites highly trained professionals who possess a history of competency to join our Licensing Program and learn to work as we do.

We acknowledge that people who seek us are usually dealing with painful issues and have gone through difficult experiences. Therefore, our programs and approach were designed to take into consideration the fact that each person is unique and singular. Our professionals are constantly honing their skills to better serve our clients with excellence and compassion.

Treatment Options:

We offer a variety of treatment modalities: weekly, bi-monthly, and one or two-day intensives for those who are traveling distances for treatment. This offers the possibility of a faster resolution and intense attention for those who prefer an accelerated rate of change. We offer therapy in three languages: Portuguese, English, and Spanish.

For more information: +55 61 3242 5826 in Brasília. www.traumaclinic.com.br or write us at: contato@traumaclinic.com.br

You can also subscribe to our YouTube channel, TraumaClinic do Brasil, where you will find EMDR sessions with English, Spanish, and Portuguese subtitles.

More Books by The Author

To purchase a paperback or e-book version of these books, please visit www.amazon.com

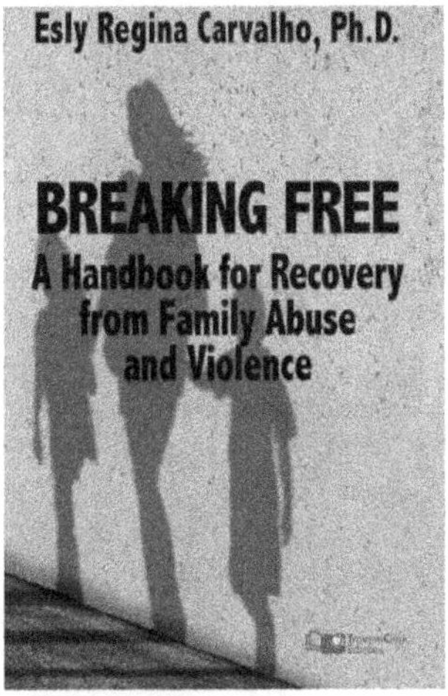

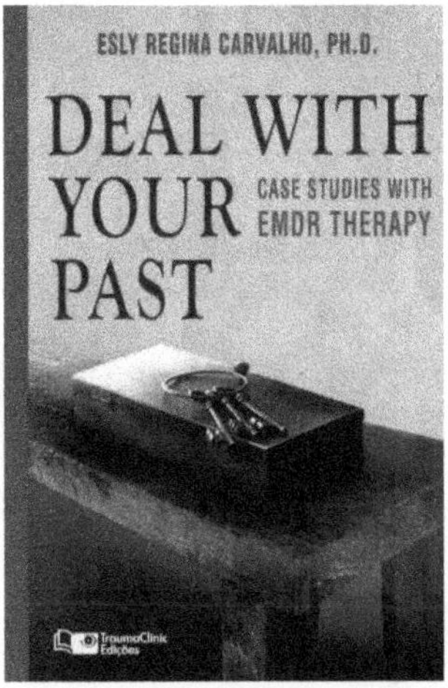

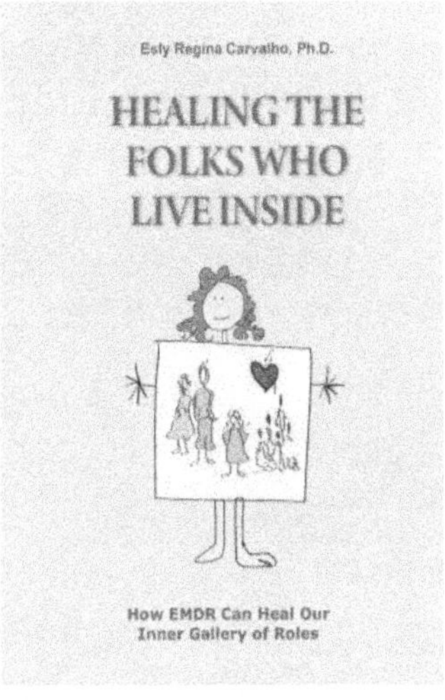

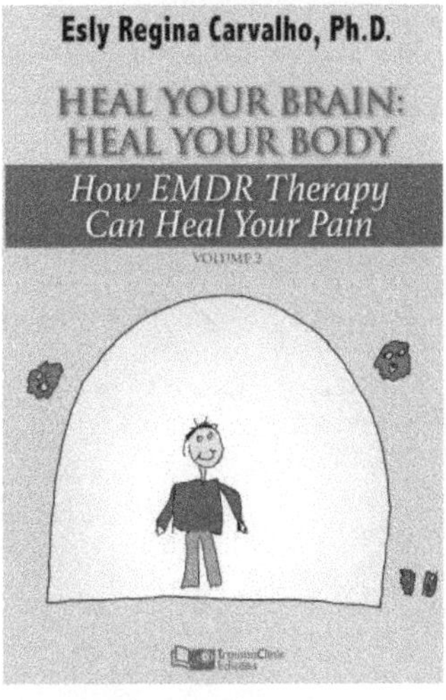

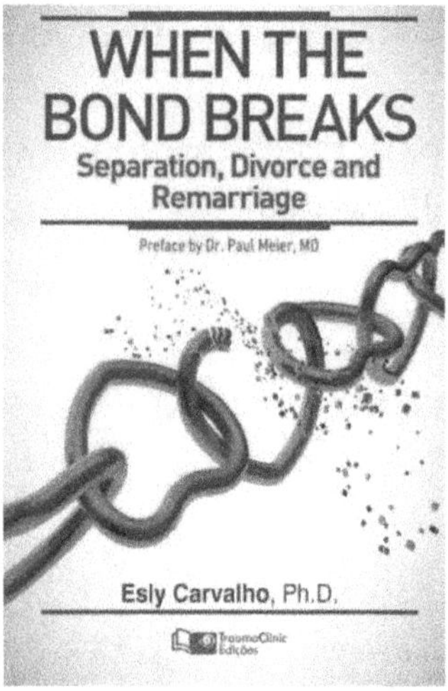

For more information visit:
www.plazacounselingservices.com

If you would like to sign up to receive our newsletter about events and publications visit the following link:
https://bit.ly/2vNR4Vc

www.ingramcontent.com/pod-product-compliance
Lightning Source LLC
Chambersburg PA
CBHW051735040426
42447CB00008B/1152